An Instant Idea Book

Building Literacy

- The Writing Process

- Journals

- Literature Charts

Written by

Barbara Gruber and Sue Gruber

Illustrated by

Mike Denman

C0-DUQ-262

© Frank Schaffer Publications, Inc.   FS-8323 Building Literacy

FS-8323 Building Literacy
ISBN # 0-86734-139-4
All rights reserved—Printed in the U.S.A.
Copyright © 1992 Frank Schaffer Publications, Inc.
1028 Via Mirabel
Palos Verdes Estates, CA 90274

Table of Contents

* Reproducible Pages

Table of Contents

* Reproducible Pages

Introduction

Building Literacy will help you create a language-rich classroom. Strategies are provided for teaching the writing process in an easy step-by-step manner. This book also contains a variety of instantly usable journal ideas and practical, simple-to-make charts that will help you bring literature to life in your classroom. We hope our ideas help your students become skilled language users.

Barbara Gruber

Sue Gruber

The Writing Process

Writing As a Process

Unlock the writer in each of your students by teaching the process of writing rather than focusing only on a final product. Students who use the writing process will become more skilled writers.

The writing process contains five steps—prewriting, drafting, revising, proofreading, and publishing. Using the process helps students become organized and effective writers. Not all of the steps in the process need to be used every time a student writes.

The steps of the writing process are outlined on pages 7 and 8. You may want to copy the steps onto a chart to post in your room for student reference or use Frank Schaffer's *The Writing Process* (FS-2400).

Model the Process

One of the best ways to teach your class the writing process is to model it. The next time you need to write a letter, demonstrate for your class the steps in the writing process. For example, tell your class you need to write a letter to the PTA requesting money for a field trip. Jot a list of words and thoughts you want to include in the letter on the chalkboard or a chart during the prewriting phase. Next, write your draft of the letter. Ask students for suggestions on how to make the letter better and do the revisions. Walk your class through the proofreading stage and finish with a letter that is ready to be sent. You may want to model the process several times throughout the year to reinforce the writing process!

The Writing Process

Steps in the Writing Process

Prewriting
Think About It
- consider who will read it and why
- form ideas
- discuss ideas with others
- read and observe
- gather and record information
- brainstorm a list of words and thoughts
- think about what you want to say
- plan how you will say it

Drafting
Write It Down
- organize your thoughts
- choose ideas and develop them
- sequence what you want to say
- write a first draft
- have others read it and offer suggestions

Revising
Make It Better
- read what you wrote
- think about what others said
- rearrange words or ideas
- add or take out parts
- change words or ideas to better ones
- complete any unfinished thoughts
- replace overused or unclear words

FS-8323 Building Literacy

The Writing Process Chart

Proofreading
Make It Correct
- make sure all sentences are complete
- check spelling, capitalization, and punctuation
- look for words not used correctly
- mark corrections needed
- have someone check your work
- recopy it correctly and neatly

Publishing
Share It With Others
- read it aloud to a person or group
- bind it in a book
- record it on tape
- display it for others to see
- talk it over with someone
- illustrate it, perform it, or set it to music
- make it part of a personal collection of your work

The Writing Process

Prewriting

Prewriting activities generate ideas and enthusiasm for writing. Prewriting activities ease students into writing by providing an opportunity to think about the topic and discuss ideas with others before writing.

Try the following prewriting activities with your class:

- Have students list topics they are interested in writing about.
- Discuss ideas and topics.
- Brainstorm a list of words and ideas about the topic, individually or as a whole class activity.
- Gather additional information about the topic.
- Decide who your writing is targeted for and how you plan to get your ideas onto paper.
- Share any information you have on the topic. What a great way to integrate literature and art with writing!

I'd like to read you a poem about trees.

Trees
branches
fall

Drafting

During the drafting stage, students begin to organize their thoughts and ideas on paper. Encourage your students to make a web or story map during this step. Ideas from the webs or maps can be sequenced and used in a first draft. During drafting, the objective is to get ideas on paper. There is time later to correct spelling and punctuation.

Once the first draft is complete, students can read one another's drafts and offer suggestions!

FS-8323 Building Literacy

The Writing Process

Revising

The revising process enables students to reread, reflect, and make changes to improve their writing. During revising, a writer does these things:

- Reads what he has written

- Adds any information he left out

- Deletes redundant parts

- Replaces unclear and overused words—with the help of a dictionary, thesaurus, or word bank

- Rearranges the sequence of events

- Reflects on feedback from others and incorporates suggestions with which he agrees

- Rereads the work aloud to make sure it flows smoothly

- Receives input from others about the revisions

Have students use the Feedback Form on page 11 when they are responding to other students' writing.

Revision Feedback Form

Writer's Name _____

An interesting part of your paper is _____

_____

I was confused when I read the part about _____

_____

The word _____ is overused. Try using _____

or _____ instead. Add more details about _____

_____

Take out the part about _____

_____

_____

_____

The ending is _____

_____

From _____ Date _____

a reproducible page
FS-8323 Building Literacy

The Writing Process

Proofreading

In the proofreading stage of the writing process, the writer focuses on making the work correct. The writer first tries to find and correct as many of his own errors as possible. Then the writer passes his paper on to a proofreading partner or group.

Proofreading Partners

Proofreading partners exchange papers with one another and check their partner's work for:

- Complete sentences
- Correct spelling, capitalization, and punctuation
- Clearly expressed ideas

After the papers have been checked, the writer makes a neat, correct copy.

Proofreading Groups

Proofreading groups consist of four students who have papers that are ready for proofreading. One student in the group is in charge of checking each paper for spelling errors only. Another student is only to correct punctuation errors. A third student checks only for capitalization errors. The fourth student reads each paper aloud in a whisper to determine if it makes sense.

The papers are rotated among the group members. By the time each student gets her paper back, it has been checked for punctuation, spelling, and capitalization errors and read aloud to make sure it makes sense. She then changes what she agrees needs to be changed and makes a final copy.

FS-8323 Building Literacy

The Writing Process

Publishing

The final step in the writing process, publishing, provides an opportunity for writers to share their writing with others! Knowing that his writing will be published can motivate the reluctant writer. Every piece of a student's writing need not published. Why not have each student periodically select a piece of writing to publish!

There are a variety of ways for students to publish and share their work:

- Bind the final copy into a book, adding illustrations if desired.

- Display the papers in the classroom for others to read and enjoy.

- Record the writing on tape.

- Read the writing to a partner or small group, or to the entire class.

- Read the writing to students in another class.

Consider having an author's chair in your classroom! A bright cushion can make any classroom chair into a special author's chair. Whenever a child shares his writing, he sits in the author's chair.

FS-8323 Building Literacy

The Writing Process

Evaluation of Writing

Evaluation of students' writing can be difficult. You want to provide enough feedback for students to improve their writing skills without suppressing their enthusiasm for writing.

Writing Conferences

Writing conferences provide an ideal opportunity for the teacher to give students feedback and encourage them to evaluate their work for themselves. Writing conferences may be held with just one student or with a small group of students. Here are some steps to follow during writing conferences:

- Each student reads his writing aloud.
- The writing is discussed.
- The teacher and/or group members provide feedback and suggestions for improvement.
- The conference is ended with a positive comment about the writing.

During or after each conference, you may want to jot notes about each student's writing progress.

Instant Evaluators

Reproduce the Instant Evaluators on page 15 and use them to evaluate your students' writing. These quick-to-use evaluators provide feedback in a positive way. Cut them apart and staple into a file folder as shown. Now your Instant Evaluators are easy to keep track of and use!

Teacher Evaluation

The reproducible Teacher Evaluation Checklist on page 16 provides an easy way to let students know the strong points as well as the areas that need improvement in their writing. You may wish to complete this checklist during a writing conference with a student.

Student Evaluation

Encourage students to evaluate their own writing and they will become more actively involved in the writing process. The reproducible Student Evaluation Checklist on page 16 is perfect for students to use when evaluating their own writing.

Idea

Use a highlighting marker to show students which parts of their papers are examples of excellent work. Highlighting a sentence or two is a quick way to emphasize the positive aspects of students' writing.

Writer's Name _____

The strong points of your paper are _____

_____

_____

Your paper can be improved by _____

_____

_____

From _____ Date _____

Your paper is:
- ☐ neat
- ☐ creative
- ☐ organized
- ☐ interesting
- ☐ _____

Your paper was checked for:
- ☐ spelling
- ☐ capitalization
- ☐ punctuation
- ☐ creative ideas
- ☐ content
- ☐ _____

Your paper needs:
- ☐ to be neater
- ☐ correct spelling
- ☐ complete sentences
- ☐ more details
- ☐ capitalization
- ☐ punctuation
- ☐ _____

To the author: Your book has:
- ☐ beautiful illustrations
- ☐ an attractive cover
- ☐ interesting sentences
- ☐ _____

and is fun to read

FS-8323 Building Literacy

Student Evaluation Checklist

My Name _____

Writing Project _____

Date Evaluated _____

Names of proofreading partner or group _____

I got ready to write this paper by _____

I chose this topic because _____

I revised my work with help from _____

I shared my finished work with _____

The best part of this writing is _____

I'd like to improve by _____

My plans for my next writing project are _____

Teacher Evaluation Checklist

Student Name _____

Writing Project _____

Date _____

	Super	Good	Needs Work
Ideas: Clear, easy to understand			
Content: Ideas follow topic			
Organization: Beginning, middle, end			
Vocabulary: A variety of words used			
Usage: Words used correctly			
Spelling: Words spelled correctly			
Capitalization: Used correctly			
Punctuation: Used correctly			
Handwriting: Easy to read			

Comments: _____

FS-8323 Building Literacy

The Writing Process

Writing Activities

Think about the reasons people write. The purpose of writing is to communicate. Students are motivated to write when they are writing for a purpose. Provide some "real" writing experiences for your students to enjoy!

Letters

Students can write letters to their families, friends, pen pals, authors of favorite books, and newspaper editors. Letters are fun to write and responses are exciting to receive.

Lists

Help your students get organized by having them jot down things they have to do. Encourage students to keep a running list of books they enjoy. Students can share lists with friends and suggest books they might enjoy.

Notes

Have students write reminder notes to themselves when they need to remember to bring something important to school. Suggest that students write you a short note when they have something to tell you.

FS-8323 Building Literacy

The Writing Process

Thank-you Notes

Let students write thank-you notes to the custodian, cook, and librarian, to other classes that have done something special, and to classroom volunteers and guest speakers. These thank-you notes are sure to brighten the day of helpful people at your school!

Interviews

Have each student interview an important person in his life. First the student writes interview questions. Then, during the interview with the special person, the student writes the response to each question. The interviews are then shared with the class.

Articles

Encourage students to write articles or stories to contribute to a class or school newsletter. Writing for publication in a newsletter is exciting!

The Writing Process

Books

Books are fun for students to write! Make student books by stapling sheets of writing and drawing paper together. Add a construction paper cover. Students copy in the books stories they have written. Illustrations are added and the books are placed in the classroom library for everyone to enjoy!

Directions

Have students write directions for getting from the classroom to the school office, library, or cafeteria. Let students exchange directions and follow them to see if they are correct. Make a booklet of school directions for new students.

Advertisements

Consider using a bulletin board in your classroom for student-created advertisements. Students can write advertisements for the following:

- Lost or found items
- Toys or books they are willing to trade with other students
- Help they need on a project
- An area of expertise they are willing to share with others

FS-8323 Building Literacy

The Writing Process

Writing Portfolios

Copies of all published writing are kept in each student's writing portfolio. Portfolios can be construction paper folders or file folders. It is important that all writing placed in the portfolio be dated. You might want to provide a date stamp and let students stamp their completed writing. Inside the front cover of his portfolio, each student records the title and date of each piece of writing placed in the portfolio. The portfolio becomes a sequential record of each student's writing progress throughout the school year.

The writing portfolio is ideal to share with parents during conferences when discussing writing progress and performance.

Portfolios tend to get lost or damaged when stored in students' desks. It's a good idea to collect the portfolios and store them in a box.

Idea

You may want to make several portfolios for each student. Consider making math, science, and reading portfolios. Store the portfolios in empty cereal boxes, as shown.

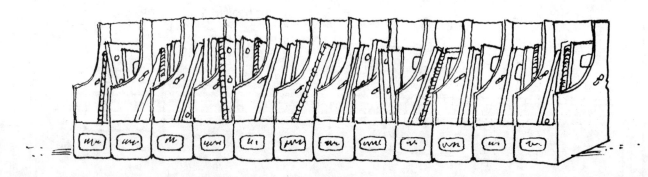

The Writing Process

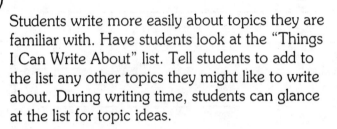

Writing Folders

A writing folder helps students organize
and plan their writing. Make a writing folder
for each child in your class. Reproduce
pages 22 and 23 and paste them inside
each folder as shown.

Students write more easily about topics they are
familiar with. Have students look at the "Things
I Can Write About" list. Tell students to add to
the list any other topics they might like to write
about. During writing time, students can glance
at the list for topic ideas.

Have students bring their writing folders to writing
conferences. Ask each child if there is a specific skill
she would like to focus on. Add the skill to the "As a
writer, I ..." list. You may add skills to the list that
each child needs more practice with. Tell your students
to get in the habit of checking their work against the
"As a writer, I ..." list. Once a child feels she has
mastered, for example, using capitals at the beginning
of sentences, she checks that skill off and focuses
on the next skill she needs to master.

The "Proofreading Marks" and "Check Your Work" lists are handy for students to use during the
proofreading step of the writing process. You may want to copy them onto wall charts or use
Frank Schaffer's *Proofreading Marks* (FS-2467) and *Check Your Work* (FS-2361).

Using Writing Folders

Students keep their in-progress writing inside their writing folders. Every week or two, students
choose a piece of writing to publish. Completed, ready-to-publish work is moved from the writing
folder to the writing portfolio.

my friends

Things I Can Write About

☐ myself _____
☐ my family _____
☐ my friends _____
☐ my school _____

my hobby

☐ _____
☐ _____
☐ _____
☐ _____
☐ _____
☐ _____
☐ _____
☐ _____
☐ _____

☐ _____
☐ _____
☐ _____
☐ _____
☐ _____
☐ _____
☐ _____
☐ _____

Name _____

As a writer, I
☐ use capitals to begin sentences.
☐ end sentences with punctuation marks.
☐ _____
☐ _____
☐ _____
☐ _____
☐ _____
☐ _____
☐ _____
☐ _____

FS-8323 Building Literacy

Proofreading Marks

Mark	What It Means
¶	Start a new paragraph. Indent the paragraph.
⌄	Insert letters or words.
ℒ	Take out words, sentences, and punctuation marks.
/	Change to a small letter.
☰	Change to a capital letter.

Check Your Work

1. Is your name on your paper?

2. Did you follow all directions?

3. Is your work neat?

4. Does each sentence begin with a capital letter?

5. Do other important words need capital letters?

6. Does each sentence end with correct punctuation?

7. Is each word spelled correctly?

8. Is each sentence a complete thought?

a reproducible page

FS-8323 Building Literacy

Journals

Journal Writing

To build writing fluency, students need frequent opportunities to write for authentic purposes. Journals provide valuable writing experiences for the developing writers in your classroom.

Making Journals

Make a booklet from lined writing paper with construction paper or wallpaper covers. Staple the pages together.

Students can use commercially bound "blank books" they bring from home.

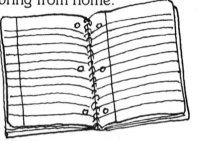

Use composition books.

Use a loose-leaf binder. Pages can be added as needed.

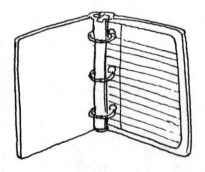

Organizational Ideas for Journals

Divide students' names into five groups. Assign each group a different color. Have students color-code their journals by making a colored dot on the upper right-hand corner of the cover. Collect and read journals from a different group each day. By the end of the week, you will have read each student's journal.

Store journals in a box or basket instead of in students' desks.

Journals

Scheduling Journal Writing

When should students write in journals?
It is a good idea to have a certain time of day when students write in their journals. Why not have students place their journals on their desks before recess? Then they will be ready to begin writing when they come back into the classroom.

How often should students write in journals?
Start with two or three times a week before making it a daily activity. Respond to your students' interests; if daily journal writing is getting tiresome for students, do it less often.

How much time should be allotted to journal writing?
Provide five to ten minutes when you first start journals with your students. Gradually increase the time. Since students are going to finish writing at different times, it's a good idea to tell students what you want them to do when they have finished writing.

Kinds of Journals

Personal Journals (pages 30–32)
Students write about feelings and/or events at school or outside of school.

Literature Journals (pages 33–34)
Students respond to literature in their journals.

Diaries, Learning Logs, and Theme Journals (pages 35–36)
Students write about a classroom topic.

Ideas

- Journal writing can be a free-time activity. When students have extra time, they can choose to add to their journals.

- Provide a date stamp so students can record the date on their journal entries.

Today is February 3rd!

Journals

Topics for Journals

Student-Selected Content
Students can write freely about any topic.

Teacher-Selected Topic
Students write on a topic provided by the teacher.

Suggested Topics
Students can write about a topic they choose. The teacher suggests a topic for students who are having difficulty thinking of something to write about.

Pick a Topic
Jot writing topics on strips of tagboard, craft sticks, or index cards. Put them in an envelope or container. Select a topic and jot it on the chalkboard for students to use if they wish. Do not place that topic back in the container until all topics have been used.

| April | | | | |
Monday	Tuesday	Wednesday	Thursday	Friday
When someone plays a trick on me, I feel . . .	A Holiday I Would Change	Copy a definition from the dictionary.	Write a definition for WOOZLE.	Invent a list of new words from A to Z.
Bicycle Rules	The Bicycle Mystery	My Long List of Colors	All About Rabbits	The Missing Easter Eggs
My Long List of Birds	The Bird Who Couldn't Sing	What if it rained for 40 days and 40 nights?	What if it never rained?	**Tall Tales** The sky is blue because Mr. Sun hangs out his blue blanket each day.
Give examples of beauty.	Copy the first sentence from three different storybooks.	Write your own first sentence for three different books.	Write a story using one of your first sentences.	How I'm Doing in School This Year
My Favorite Clothes	Compare your shoe with your shirt.	What would happen if everyone wore the same clothes?	Design a new thing to wear. Describe it.	**Word Box** showers nest flowers bunny basket sunshine

Frank Schaffer's *Daily Writing Activities* (FS-8482)

Post a Calendar
Post a calendar of daily writing activities for the month. Prepare your own calendar or use Frank Schaffer's *Daily Writing Activities* or *Daily Writing Calendars*. Students who need a subject for writing can choose one from the calendar.

Create a List of Ideas
Have students staple a piece of lined paper inside the covers of their journals. Brainstorm a "Things I Know About" list with students. Jot the ideas on the chalkboard for students to copy. When students need a topic for writing, they can glance at the list for ideas. From time to time, brainstorm additional topics for students to add to their lists.

FS-8323 Building Literacy

Journals

Responding to Journals

The purpose of journal writing is to build writing fluency. There are many ways you can respond to students' journals. And there are many ways students can share their journals. The purpose of responding to students' writing is to offer encouragement to developing writers and to show acceptance of their writing. Students can freely express their ideas in writing, knowing their writing will not be criticized, edited, or graded. Respond to your students' journals in the following ways:

- Hold conferences with students. Confer with a different student each day. Keep track on a class list to make sure you hold a conference with each student.

- After reading students' journal entries, jot comments on stick-on notes. Place the notes in students' journals.

- Have students staple an extra piece of lined paper inside the front covers of their journals to use as a "Comment Page." Write your responses on the "Comment Page" instead of on the student's page.

Journals

Sharing Journals

- Assign each student to a journal partner. Have students read journal entries to partners. Reassign partners every few weeks.

- Assign students to journal-sharing groups of three or four students each. Let students take turns reading journal entries to their groups. Reassign groups every few weeks.

- Read and discuss journal entries during a conference with each student.

- Assign each student to a partner for a journal exchange. First students write in their own journals. Then, when it is time for journal writing again, students exchange journals with their partners. Each student reads his partner's entry and writes a response in his partner's journal. Students continue alternating between writing in their own journals and reading and responding to a partner's journal. The journal exchange adds variety to journal writing. You may want to have a journal exchange for a few weeks and then discontinue it. Then at another time, assign new partners and resume the exchange for a few more weeks.

FS-8323 Building Literacy

Journals

Spelling

Encourage students to use invented spellings when they write in journals. If you help students spell words, they end up waiting for spelling help instead of writing freely.

Ideas

- You may wish to call invented spelling "temporary spelling" or "transitional spelling." These terms are more easily understood and accepted by parents.

- Show your students how to use "magic writing." When they are having difficulty with a word, tell them to write the beginning letter (or letters) and then to save a space for the word by making a line as shown. Students can add the ending letters if they know them. Students save a long space for long words and shorter spaces for short words. When students use magic writing, they can keep on writing and get help with their spelling later. Because students continue writing, the missing words will be in context and can be filled in later. If you are circulating and notice magic writing, offer help to the student.

The Teacher's Journal

When students write in their journals, you should write in your journal also. When you write and share your writing, it adds importance to journal writing and establishes you as a "fellow writer." You can participate in the journal-sharing activities suggested on page 28.

Journals

Getting Started With Personal Journals

Provide support and encouragement by letting students begin personal journal writing as a class activity. Prewriting discussions and writing as a group will help students build confidence for later independent writing. Begin a class journal on Monday and finish it on Friday. Use a piece of 12" x 18" paper for each day of the week. On Monday, toward the end of the school day, hold a class discussion about the events of the day. Then tell students you want to write a few sentences about the day's happenings in the class journal. Write the date at the top of the page. Record a few sentences dictated by students. Read the entry aloud. Then have students reread it aloud. Do this each day. On Friday, staple the pages together and add covers to make a journal. Students will enjoy reading this record of class events.

The following week, make another class journal and give each student a five-page writing booklet. At the end of each day, discuss the day's events and write a sentence in the class journal. Then have students write a sentence in their booklets. Students can copy the sentence you wrote in the class journal or write their own sentences. At the end of the week, you will have a class journal and each student will have an individual journal. Each day, ask a few volunteers to share their writing.

The group journal writing activity described above will prepare students to begin journal writing on their own.

Adding Variety to Journals

The following suggestions will add interest to journal writing and increase students' motivation:

- Have students make lists instead of writing sentences. They may want to make a list of things they like, things they want to accomplish over the weekend, places they would like to visit, or favorite foods.
- Have students draw pictures instead of writing.
- Suggest that students write riddles or poems.
- Encourage students to practice letter writing in their journals.

Journals

Creating a Print-Rich Environment

Journal writing will be easier for students if they are surrounded by print. Create "Words for Writing" charts with your class. Choose a familiar topic and brainstorm a list of words with your students. Write the words on a chart and post it in the classroom. Some sample "Words for Writing" charts are shown below and on page 32. It is important that you elicit the words for your charts from your students.

You can also generate a list of sentence starters for a writing topic and list them on the chalkboard. Students may use their own ideas or sentence starters from the list.

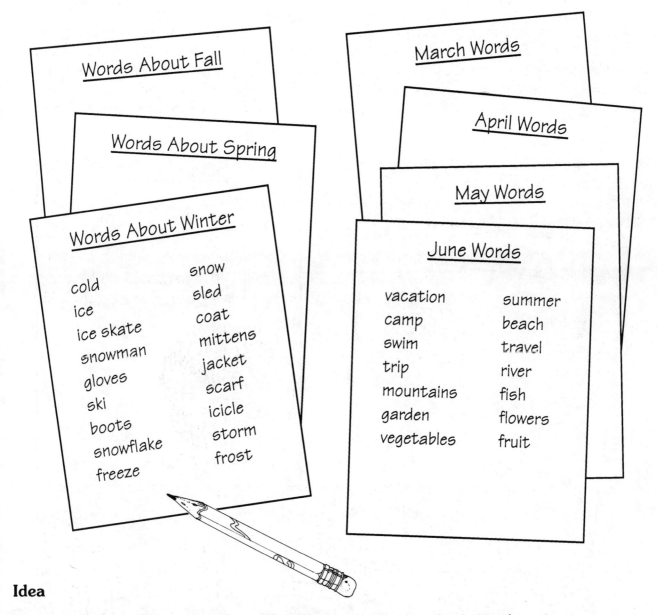

Words About Fall

Words About Spring

Words About Winter

cold
ice
ice skate
snowman
gloves
ski
boots
snowflake
freeze

snow
sled
coat
mittens
jacket
scarf
icicle
storm
frost

March Words

April Words

May Words

June Words

vacation
camp
swim
trip
mountains
garden
vegetables

summer
beach
travel
river
fish
flowers
fruit

Idea

Fasten several word charts together with binder rings to make a big book of words.

Journals

Words About Pets

dog
kitten
fish
cage
aquarium
eat
play

cat
puppy
bird
turtle
food
sleep

Words About Literature

cover
title
story
illustrations
characters
middle

author
pages
setting
plot
beginning
end

School Words

reading
writing
science
social studies
teachers
student
principal
library
lunch
classroom

math
art
music
books
pencils
desks
recess
office
bus

Family Words

mother
father
aunt
cousin
grandmother
stepdad
relatives
play
eat

brother
sister
uncle
mom
dad
baby
work
relax
sleep

FS-8323 Building Literacy

Journals

Literature Journals

Discuss literature journal writing with your students and model writing in a class literature journal before asking students to begin individual literature journals.

Class Literature Journals

After reading a chapter aloud each day, discuss the chapter and elicit from the class a few sentences about the chapter. Write the sentences in a class literature journal. Before reading the next chapter aloud, read the last journal entry to the class. It refreshes everyone's memory about where the story left off and gets everyone ready to hear the next chapter.

> Let's read what we wrote in the journal yesterday. Then I'll read the next chapter.

Chapter 6
Stuart rode the bus to the park.
He sailed a boat and won the race.
Chapter 7

After creating a class literature journal, have students make individual literature journals to go with the next book you read aloud. Continue to provide class discussion and a group writing activity after each chapter. Read aloud the first chapter. Discuss the chapter and write a few dictated sentences about the chapter on the chalkboard. Then have students write about the chapter. After students write about the chapter, let them draw a picture on the page. Have students do this for each chapter. When the book is finished, students can staple their pages in sequence and add covers to make a journal about the book.

FS-8323 Building Literacy

Journals

Adding Variety to Literature Journals

Have students draw

- a place in the story
- a character
- a gift for a character

Have students predict

- what will happen next
- how the story will end

Have students write about characters telling

- how they think characters feel
- if characters remind them of themselves
- if characters remind them of someone they know
- why they would like to have a character as a friend
- how a character could change the story
- how a character has changed throughout the story
- why they like or dislike characters
- what happened from the first-person viewpoint of a character

Have students write notes about books

- to the teacher
- to a story character
- to the book's author
- from one character to another

Have students write an evaluation of the book.

I think everyone should read this book!

Journals

A Class Diary

A diary is a type of journal. Keep a class diary with your students. This will provide a good record of classroom events. Begin with a blank calendar grid on a large piece of tagboard or butcher paper. Then, at the end of each day, write on the calendar a sentence or two about the day.

Ideas

• Have K–1 students dictate a sentence for the teacher to write.

• Have students in grades 2 through 6 take turns writing on the class diary grid.

• Use binder rings to fasten completed diary pages into a book. At the end of the year, take the book apart and display the pages around the classroom. Students enjoy reading and reflecting on the school year. If students are making yearbooks, they can get ideas for their yearbooks from the class diary.

A Learning Log

A learning log is a record of information and skills that a student has learned. You may wish to have students keep this type of journal to reinforce important learning experiences. At the end of each day, ask students to write a sentence in their learning logs about the most important things they learned that day. Another option is to have students write an entry at the end of each week.

FS-8323 Building Literacy

Journals

Theme Journals

Theme journals add value to the study of any theme. K–1 students can dictate sentences for the teacher to record. Students in grades 2–6 can keep individual theme journals.

- Brainstorm a cluster of words about the theme your class is studying. Write the words on a chart. As the class comes across new words that go with the theme, add them to the chart. Students can use the chart to get ideas and to learn the correct spelling of words related to the theme.

- Have students decorate covers of their theme journals with illustrations about the theme.

- Have students make a "Things I Already Know" page for listing information they know about the theme.

- Have students make a "Things I Want to Find Out" page for jotting down questions about the theme.

- Have students keep learning logs (page 35).

- Students can add to their theme journals samples of work done during the theme study. At the end of the theme study, they will have both a journal and a scrapbook about the theme.

Literature Charts

Using Literature Charts

Use literature charts to increase your students' understanding and appreciation of literature. Try them with your whole class or with cooperative groups, partners, or individual students. You'll be amazed at their versatility!

Benefits of Multipurpose Literature Charts

- They enable you to link oral language, writing, and reading.
- They help students organize and synthesize information.
- They provide a focus for discussions.
- They create a print-rich environment in your classroom.

Ways to Display Charts

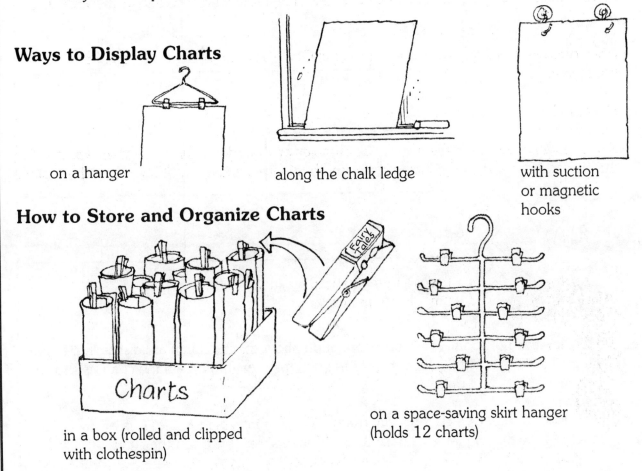

on a hanger

along the chalk ledge

with suction or magnetic hooks

How to Store and Organize Charts

in a box (rolled and clipped with clothespin)

on a space-saving skirt hanger (holds 12 charts)

Ideas

Laminate your charts to make them last.

As you use a chart, take a moment to jot your teaching ideas on the back of the chart.

When you need multiple copies of a chart, make one sample and have an aide or parent helper make the extras for you. This can be an at-home task for a parent or other volunteer.

Literature Charts

Story Discussion Chart

Use a story discussion chart with any story or book at all grade levels! This chart adds value to postreading discussions.

Who found the golden ticket?

Charlie and the Chocolate Factory by Roald Dahl				
Who	Did What	When	Where	Why
	found a golden ticket			
Mr. Wonka				
			in the chocolate factory	
	sang a song			
Augustus Gloop				

Using a Story Discussion Chart

Fill in one box in each horizontal row with information about the book you are discussing. If you are discussing *Charlie and the Chocolate Factory,* you might want to fill in the chart as shown above.

Grades K–6: Use the chart as a class activity. Read aloud the information that is presented. Ask students to supply the missing information. Record students' responses on the chart.

Grades 2–6: Use the chart with cooperative learning groups. Divide your class into four or five groups. Give each group a Story Discussion Chart. Have group members discuss and record missing information on the chart. Group members can take turns assuming the roles of Reader, Writer, and Checker.

Grades 3–6: Make the chart on an 8½" x 11" piece of paper, filling in one box in each horizontal row. Reproduce the chart for each student or pair of students. Have students fill in the missing information about the story.

Literature Charts

Story Discussion Chart

Who	Did What	When	Where	Why

Sarah, Plain and Tall

Use Story Discussion Charts for

- ✓ Grades K–6
- ✓ Any story
- ✓ Books with chapters
- ___ Prereading activity
- ___ Activity as you read
- ✓ Postreading
- ✓ Whole-class discussion
- ✓ Cooperative learning groups
- ✓ Pairs of students
- ✓ Individual students

Ideas

- Instead of filling in the information in one box in each row, as shown on the chart on page 38, elicit this information from students.

- Add additional lines to the chart to extend the activity.

Literature Charts

Story Web Charts

Story webs help students develop a "sense of story." Understanding story structure enables students to make predictions and understand what they read, and helps them write original stories.

Using a Story Web Chart

Make one of the charts shown on page 41. Choose the story web that best suits the needs of your class.

Grades K–4: Use the chart for a class activity. Elicit from students information for the web. Record the information on the chart.

Grades 2–4: Use the chart with cooperative learning groups. Divide your class into groups of three to five students. Give each group a Story Web Chart and have students in the group write their names on the chart. The goal of the group is to complete the chart. The students discuss the story and record information on the chart. Let students write and/or draw about the story. Then have each group share its chart.

Grades 2–6: Display a Story Web Chart for students to copy. Then have students make and complete a similar web on 12" x 18" paper.

Grades 3–4: Instead of making a large chart, make the web on an 8½" x 11" piece of paper. Reproduce the chart for each student or pair of students. Have students complete webs about stories they read.

Literature Charts

Story Web Chart

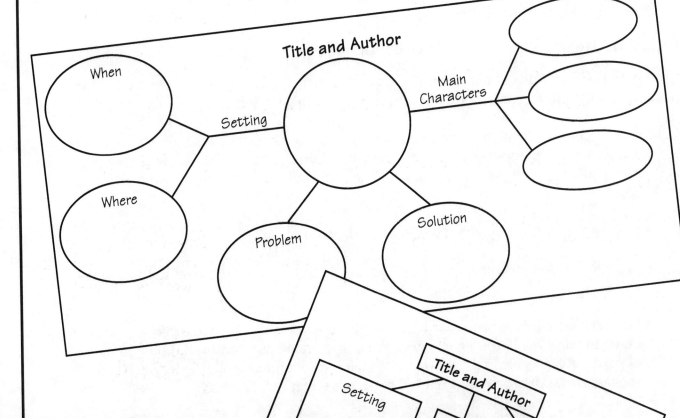

Title and Author

When

Setting

Where

Main Characters

Problem

Solution

Title and Author

Setting

Plot

Characters

Beginning

Middle

End

Use Story Web Charts for

- ✓ Grades K–6
- ✓ Any story
- ✓ Books with chapters
- ___ Prereading activity
- ✓ Activity as you read
- ✓ Postreading
- ✓ Whole-class discussion
- ✓ Cooperative learning groups
- ✓ Pairs of students
- ✓ Individual students

FS-8323 Building Literacy

Literature Charts

"Read, Think, and Write" Charts

"Read, Think, and Write" charts provide a writing frame for your students to complete after reading a book or hearing a story.

Using a "Read, Think, and Write" Chart

Grades K–1: Choose one of the writing frame charts to use with your class. Write it on chart paper or copy it on the chalkboard. Elicit information from students and record it.

Grades 2–6: Choose a writing frame to use with your class. Lead students through the writing activity, discussing their ideas as you follow the pattern on the chart. This whole-class activity will familiarize students with using writing frames. Then let students work in one of the following ways:

- Display the writing frame that you want students to complete independently.

- Place four different writing frames on the chalk ledge. Let each student choose one to complete.

- Place students in four cooperative learning groups. Give each group a different writing frame to complete. Group members discuss their frame and complete it on one piece of paper. All students in the group write their names on the group's paper. Then a spokesperson for each group reads the group's writing to the class.

How did the story start?

Title Bread and Jam for Frances
Author Russell Hoban
The story is about a badger who won't eat anything without jam.
At the beginning _____
_____
Then _____
_____
At the end _____
_____

Literature Charts

"Read, Think, and Write" Charts

Plot

Title _____

Author _____

The problem in the story is _____

_____

_____

It was solved by _____

Setting

Title _____

Author _____

The story takes place _____

_____

_____

Characters

Title _____

Author _____

Two characters in the story _____

are _____ and _____

_____ is
(name)

_____
(what the character is like)

_____ is
(name)

_____
(what the character is like)

Sequence

Title _____

Author _____

The story is about _____

_____

At the beginning _____

_____

Then _____

At the end _____

Use "Read, Think, and Write" Charts for

- ✓ Grades K–6
- ✓ Any story
- ✓ Books with chapters
- ___ Prereading activity
- ✓ Activity as you read
- ✓ Postreading
- ✓ Whole-class discussion
- ✓ Cooperative learning groups
- ✓ Pairs of students
- ✓ Individual students

Frog and Toad are Friends

Mrs. Frisby and the Rats of Nimh

Literature Charts

Story Comparison Chart

Use comparison charts to help students understand story structure. Students can compare and contrast stories. Comparison charts can also be used to help students understand story themes.

Title	A Chair for My Mother	Ox-Cart Man
Setting	in a city	New England town in 1800's
Characters	Mama daughter Grandma Aunt Ida	mother father daughter son
Problem	Mama's feet hurt	need to provide for the family's needs
Attempts to solve problem	girl saves money to buy chair for her mother	everyone works to make goods to sell
Solution	they buy a beautiful chair	the father takes goods to market to earn money for the family
How characters felt at the end of the story	happy to be together and happy the mother likes the chair	happy to see the father come home
Theme	Families care about each other. Families work together.	

Using a Story Comparison Chart

After reading a book aloud, or after your class finishes reading a book, discuss the story and fill in the chart. Read another book and fill in the chart. Then compare and contrast the two stories.

To help students understand story themes, choose two books that have the same theme. Read one book, fill in the chart, and ask students to tell what the book was about in a few words. Then read, discuss, and fill in the chart about the other book. Ask students what that book was about. Students will understand that two very different stories can have the same theme.

Literature Charts

Story Comparison Chart

Title		
Setting		
Characters		
Problem		
Attempts to solve problem		
Solution		
How characters felt at the end of the story		
Theme		

Use Story Comparison Charts for

✓ Grades K–6
✓ Any story
✓ Books with chapters
___ Prereading activity
___ Activity as you read
✓ Postreading
✓ Whole-class discussion
✓ Cooperative learning groups
___ Pairs of students
___ Individual students

Ideas

- Make space on the chart for writing about three books instead of two.
- Record information using a different color pen for each book. This makes the information about each book stand out clearly.

© Frank Schaffer Publications, Inc.

Literature Charts

Folklore Charts

Explore the world of fairy tales and folktales with your students. Use one of the folklore charts to enhance your students' appreciation of this genre.

Using Folklore Chart A (This chart helps students compare different stories.)

Grades K–6: After reading a story, elicit information from students to write on the chart. When you have information about several stories on the chart, discuss similarities and differences found in the stories.

Tell me about a magical event.

The World of Folklore				
Title	Good Characters	Evil Characters	Magical Events	Theme
Jack and the Beanstalk				
Little Red Riding Hood				
Cinderella				

Grades 2–6: Divide your class into groups. Assign a different story to each group. Have each group discuss its story and fill in the information about it on the chart.

Using Folklore Chart B (This chart helps students compare different versions of a story.)

Grades K–6: Gather different versions of the same story. Read each version aloud and elicit from your class information for the chart.

Folklore Around the World				
Title	Country of Origin	Good Characters	Evil Characters	Magic Events
Cinderella (Perrault)	France	Cinderella Prince	Stepsisters Stepmother	Fairy Godmother uses wand
The Brocaded Slipper (Vuong)	Vietnam			

FS-8323 Building Literacy

Literature Charts

Folklore Chart A				
Title	Good Characters	Evil Characters	Magical Events	Theme

Use Folklore Chart A for

✓ Grades K–6
___ Any story
___ Books with chapters
___ Prereading activity
✓ Activity as you read
✓ Postreading
✓ Whole-class discussion
✓ Cooperative learning groups
✓ Pairs of students
✓ Individual students

Folklore Chart B				
Title	Country of Origin	Good Characters	Evil Characters	Magical Events

Use Folklore Chart B for

✓ Grades K–6
___ Any story
___ Books with chapters
___ Prereading activity
___ Activity as you read
✓ Postreading
✓ Whole-class discussion
✓ Cooperative learning groups
✓ Pairs of students
✓ Individual students

FS-8323 Building Literacy

Literature Charts

Story Map Charts

Story map charts help students enjoy and understand what they read as they read it. And at the end of the book, students have a record of the book to keep and enjoy.

Using a Story Map Chart

Grades K–3: Make Story Map Chart A to use with a book you plan to read to your class. After reading the story aloud, hold a class discussion about the book. Elicit sentences about the setting, characters and character traits, and plot to write on the chart.

Grades 1–3: Give each student a copy of Story Map Chart A. (Suggestion: Use 12" x 18" construction paper.) After students read a story, have them write sentences and draw pictures about the story on their charts. Before asking students to complete individual story map charts, it is a good idea to complete one as a class activity as described above.

Grades 2–6: Make Story Map Chart B to use with a book you plan to read to your class. If the book has 12 chapters, make 12 writing boxes on the chart in addition to the *Title, Author,* and *Characters* boxes. Number the chapter boxes. After reading each chapter, elicit a few sentences about the chapter to write in the corresponding box on the chart. When characters are introduced, write their names and character traits in the *Characters* box. As you learn more about the characters, add additional traits after their names.

Grades 2–6: Group students in cooperative learning groups of three or four students. Give each group a copy of Story Map Chart B. After your class has read a chapter in a book, have students meet in groups to discuss the chapter. Then have each group record a sentence about the most important event in the chapter and draw a picture about the chapter. Let group members take turns as recorders and illustrators. Provide opportunities for groups to share their charts with the class. Display the story map charts in the classroom.

Grades 2–6: Give each student a copy of Story Map Chart B with a chapter box for each chapter in the book they are reading. After reading each chapter, have students write a sentence on the chart telling the most important thing that happened in the chapter. Then let students make an illustration in the box for that chapter. Have students record characters and character traits in the *Characters* section. Give students opportunities to share their story map charts with partners or small groups.

Make the Story Map Chart shown on page 49 that best suits your students' needs and the book you are reading.

FS-8323 Building Literacy

Literature Charts

Use Story Map Charts for

- ✓ Grades K–6
- ✓ Any story
- ✓ Books with chapters
- ☐ Prereading activity
- ✓ Activity as you read
- ✓ Postreading
- ✓ Whole-class discussion
- ✓ Cooperative learning groups
- ✓ Pairs of students
- ✓ Individual students

Story Map Chart A

Title	Author
Setting	Characters

Beginning	Middle	End

Story Map Chart B

Title		Author			
Characters					
1	2	3	4	5	6
7	8	9	10	11	12

Ideas

- Add a section at the bottom of a story map chart where students can evaluate the book.
- Encourage students to reread story map charts for enjoyment.
- Post a story map chart that was completed as a class activity on a classroom wall or bulletin board.
- Display completed story map charts in your classroom, the office, the hallways, or the school library.

 FS-8323 Building Literacy

Literature Charts

Feelings Chart

Discussing how a story made students feel helps them feel personally connected with literature.

Using a Feelings Chart

Grades K–6: After reading, hold a class discussion about the story or chapter. Elicit the name of a story character and write it on the chart. Then ask students to name a story event involving that character for you to write on the chart. Discuss and record how the character felt and how your students feel. Continue to do this for other characters in the story.

Grades 2–6: Group your students in cooperative learning groups. Give each group a feelings chart. After reading a story or chapter, have each group discuss the story and fill in the information on the chart.

A character's name may be written on the chart more than one time if the event and feelings are different than those previously listed on the chart for that character.

The Velveteen Rabbit		by Margery Williams	
Who	What Happened?	Characters' Feelings	How We Feel
Rabbit	was a favorite toy	loved, happy	happy
Rabbit	became real	sad because he couldn't run	

I feel sorry for him!

FS-8323 Building Literacy

Literature Charts

Use Feelings Charts for

- ✓ Grades K–6
- ✓ Any story
- ✓ Books with chapters
- ___ Prereading activity
- ✓ Activity as you read
- ✓ Postreading
- ✓ Whole-class discussion
- ✓ Cooperative learning groups
- ___ Pairs of students
- ___ Individual students

Feelings Chart

Title:		Author:	
Who	What Happened?	Characters' Feelings	How We Feel

Idea

When your class has finished reading a book with chapters, have students analyze how the characters' feelings changed from the beginning of the story to the end.

FS-8323 Building Literacy

Literature Charts

"Let's Read" Charts

These charts will help get your students involved with the characters and events of a story. Use "Let's Read Charts" with a chapter book that you are reading aloud.

Using "Let's Read" Charts

Grades K–6: Make the charts shown on page 53. Choose a book with chapters to read to your class. After reading the first chapter, ask students to name characters they "met" in that chapter. Record the characters' names on the *Characters* chart. Elicit traits about the characters to list under their names. Record a sentence telling what happened in the chapter on the *Story Events* chart. Ask students to predict what will happen in the next chapter and record their predictions on the *Our Predictions* chart. If you wish, have students offer interesting quotations and new words from the story and list them on the appropriate charts. Record information on the "Let's Read" charts each time you complete a chapter.

Grades K–1: Show students the cover and pages of a picture book. Have students try to identify the characters. List the characters they suggest on the *Characters* chart. Write students' predictions of what might happen on the *Our Predictions* chart. After you read the book, see if students were correct in guessing the characters and making predictions about the story.

Literature Charts

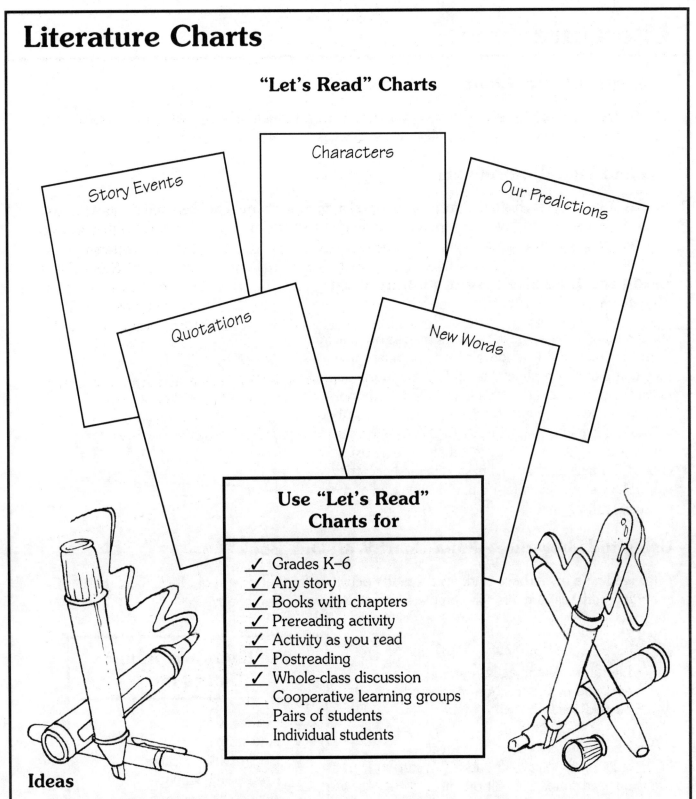

Story Events

Characters

Our Predictions

Quotations

New Words

Use "Let's Read" Charts for

✓ Grades K–6
✓ Any story
✓ Books with chapters
✓ Prereading activity
✓ Activity as you read
✓ Postreading
✓ Whole-class discussion
___ Cooperative learning groups
___ Pairs of students
___ Individual students

Ideas

• Record information on the charts each day using different colors of felt pens. For example, use blue for information about chapter two. This makes new information stand out and gives the charts more visual appeal.

• When you finish reading a book and recording on the "Let's Read" charts, arrange the charts to create a class big book. Make a title page and fasten all the pages with binder rings. Students will be eager to reread the charts.

Literature

Literature Album Chart

Your students will enjoy choosing book activities from a Literature Album Chart. Post the chart where students can easily read the suggested activities.

Student Literature Albums

Grades 2–6: Have each student make a personal literature album by folding and decorating a 12" x 18" sheet of construction paper and stapling ten sheets of paper inside. Have students number the pages from one to ten.

Using the Literature Album Chart With Ten Books

After reading a book, have students choose an activity from the chart. If they choose activity number nine, they complete it on page nine of their literature album. Have them choose a different activity for each book they read. By the time they have read ten books, they will have completed all ten of the activities and their album will be complete. Suggest that students try to choose the activity they feel best suits the book they read. Have students write the title, or title and author, on each activity page.

Using the Literature Album Chart With One Book

After reading a book, have students do all the activities for that one book. If the book has chapters, perhaps students can complete one activity after each chapter.

Ideas

- Literature Album activities can be assigned by the teacher or selected by students.

- The Literature Album is perfect for students who say "I'm done." It can be used as extra credit or with enrichment reading.

- In addition to posting the chart, you can reproduce page 55 and have students paste it inside the front cover of their album.

Use Literature Album Charts for

- ✓ Grades K–6
- ✓ Any story
- ✓ Books with chapters
- ___ Prereading activity
- ✓ Activity as you read
- ✓ Postreading
- ___ Whole-class discussion
- ___ Cooperative learning groups
- ___ Pairs of students
- ✓ Individual students

Literature Album Activities

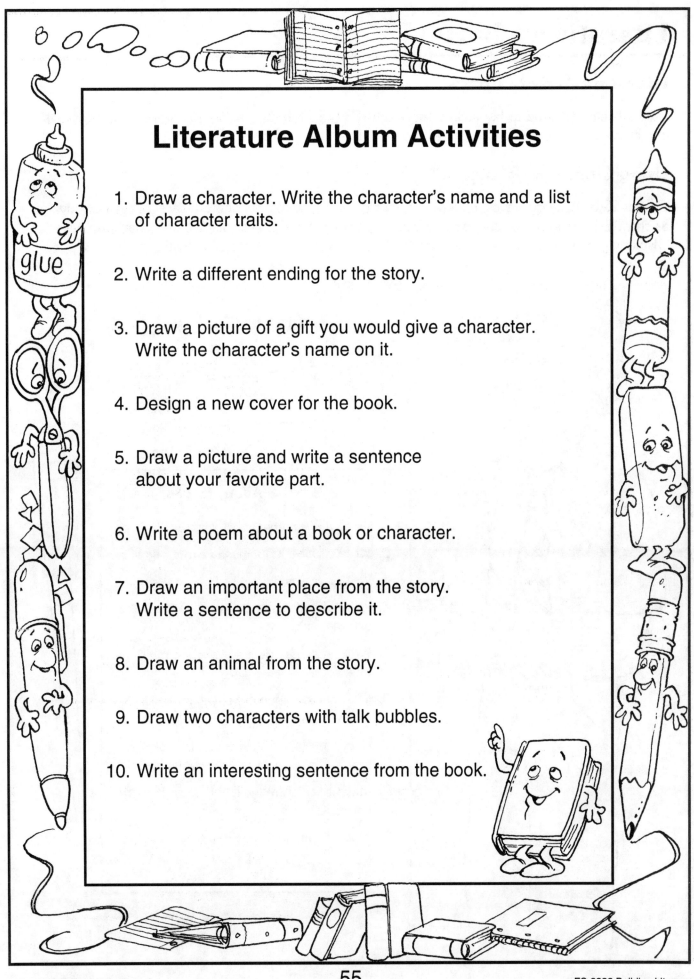

1. Draw a character. Write the character's name and a list of character traits.

2. Write a different ending for the story.

3. Draw a picture of a gift you would give a character. Write the character's name on it.

4. Design a new cover for the book.

5. Draw a picture and write a sentence about your favorite part.

6. Write a poem about a book or character.

7. Draw an important place from the story. Write a sentence to describe it.

8. Draw an animal from the story.

9. Draw two characters with talk bubbles.

10. Write an interesting sentence from the book.

FS-8323 Building Literacy

Literature Charts

Literature Activity Charts

Students can respond to books in many ways. Provide literature activity charts so your students can choose the postreading activities they feel best suit the books they read.

Using Literature Activity Charts

Grades K–6: List your favorite literature activities for students on charts. Categorize the activities as shown. Display all the charts permanently in your classroom or display one chart at a time. Displaying only one chart enables you to focus on a particular type of activity.

Literature Activity Charts

Let's Make Things About Books

Let's Talk About Books

Let's Write About Books

1. Write a poem about a character.
2. Write a letter to someone about the book.
3. Write a new ending.
4. Write about a day you would like to spend with a character.
5. Write in a diary as if you are the main character.
6. Make a list of questions you would like to ask a character.
7. Copy the first sentence of the book. Write why it is a good way to start the book.
8. Make a list of five unusual words from the book and write their meanings.
9. Write a summary of the story.
10. Write a description of the setting.

Literature Charts

Literature Activity Charts

Let's Make Things About Books

1. Make a map showing where story events take place.
2. Make a poster.
3. Make a model of something from the book.
4. Make a time line of story events.
5. Make two stick puppets of characters.
6. Make a book jacket.
7. Make a game based on the story.
8. Draw a picture of an important setting.
9. Draw two characters with talk bubbles.
10. Make a mobile.

Let's Talk About Books

1. Tell the funniest part of the story.
2. Act out a scene with a partner.
3. Retell the story.
4. Read an exciting part aloud to a partner.
5. Tell why you would recommend the book.
6. Put on a puppet show.
7. Tell about the author.
8. Tell something from the beginning, middle, and end of the story.
9. Tell another way the story could have ended.
10. Tell about something in the book that surprised you.

Use Literature Activity Charts for

- ✓ Grades K–6
- ✓ Any story
- ✓ Books with chapters
- ___ Prereading activity
- ___ Activity as you read
- ✓ Postreading
- ___ Whole-class discussion
- ___ Cooperative learning groups
- ✓ Pairs of students
- ✓ Individual students

Idea

If you want to limit students' choices to certain activities, clip a clothespin beside those activities on the chart, as shown on page 56. Ask students to choose activities marked with clothespins.

FS-8323 Building Literacy

Literature Charts

"Parts of a Book" Chart

This eye-catching chart will help your students understand the parts of a book. It will be helpful when they publish their own books in your publishing center.

Making a "Parts of a Book" Chart

To make this chart, you need to cut apart two copies of a paperback book. A book with illustrations and without chapters works best. Cut the books apart and glue the various parts of the book on a chart. Label the parts of the book.

Use a "Parts of a Book" Chart for

- ✓ Grades K–6
- ✓ Any story
- ___ Books with chapters
- ✓ Prereading activity
- ___ Activity as you read
- ✓ Postreading
- ✓ Whole-class discussion
- ___ Cooperative learning groups
- ___ Pairs of students
- ___ Individual students

Parts of a Book

Dandelion
by Don Freeman

Front Cover

Title Page

Copyright Page

Beginning of Story

Middle of Story   End of Story   Back Cover

Literature Charts

Book Questions Chart

Give your students opportunities to tell classmates about the books they read. Use the book questions chart to improve the quality of book sharing discussions.

Using a Book Questions Chart

Grades K–6: Display the chart when students are telling their classmates about books they have read and enjoyed. Encourage listeners to ask specific questions about the book. If students can't think of questions, they can use questions from the chart.

It's a good idea to have a sign-up list for students who want to tell about books. Have students sign up for book sharing once each week. Allow up to six students to sign up for each day of the week. By the end of the week, everyone will have had a chance to share a book if they wish to do so.

Book Sharing —Tuesday

1. Kyle   4. April
2. Robin   5. Sara
3. Michael   6.

Use a Book Questions Chart for

✓ Grades K–6
✓ Any story
✓ Books with chapters
___ Prereading activity
___ Activity as you read
✓ Postreading
✓ Whole-class discussion
✓ Cooperative learning groups
✓ Pairs of students
___ Individual students

Book Sharing Questions

• Who was your favorite character?
• Where can we get the book?
• What was your favorite part?
• Which illustration is your favorite?
• Where and when does the story take place?
• Would you recommend the book? Why?

The artist's name is Barbara Cooney.

Literature Charts

"Free Time" Chart

Use this chart to solve the problem of providing enrichment activities for students who say "I'm done."

Using the "Free Time" Chart

List on a chart activities students at your grade level can do when they have extra time. Tell students to choose an activity from the chart instead of saying "I'm done."

If you wish to limit choices, clip clothespins beside the activities that are available each day.

Use a "Free Time" Chart for
✓ Grades K–6
___ Any story
___ Books with chapters
___ Prereading activity
___ Activity as you read
___ Postreading
___ Whole-class discussion
___ Cooperative learning groups
✓ Pairs of students
✓ Individual students

"Free Time" Chart

- Read a book.
- Work on your literature album.
- Write in your journal.
- Clean up our classroom library.
- Work on the book you are publishing.
- Look through your writing portfolio.
- Play a reading game.
- Write a note to the teacher.
- Make a bookmark.

Literature Charts

Graph Chart

Assemble a class graph to help students connect with literature. For example, before or after reading a story about pets, make a graph about students' pets.

Using a Bar Graph Chart

Draw the grid for a graph on chart paper. Make a slit in each square. Write your students' names on squares of paper that fit in the squares on the graph. File students' names in alphabetical order in a small box. Write the graph title and choices on papers and clip these to the graph.

Grades K–6: Discuss the graph topic with your class. Have students attach their name squares on the graph with a paper clip to indicate their choice. When all names are on the graph, hold a class discussion about the information shown. When you are done with the graph, remove the name cards and labels and file the cards to use for another graphing activity.

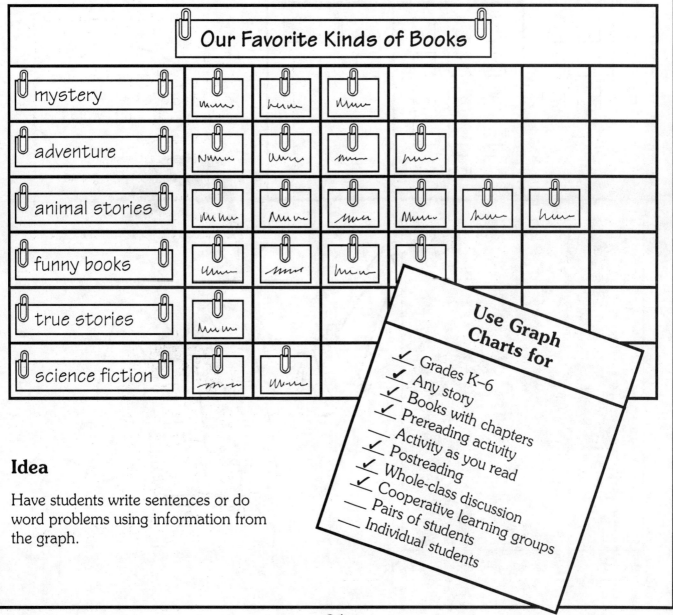

Idea

Have students write sentences or do word problems using information from the graph.

Literature Charts

Skills Chart

Use this type of chart to keep track of skills you have introduced through literature.

Using a Skills Chart

Grades K–6: Jot the skills you need to teach at your grade level on stick-on notes. Place the notes in the *Needed Skills* column of your chart. After you introduce a skill, move that stick-on note over to the *Introduced* column. After focusing on that skill another time, move the stick-on note into the *Reinforced* column. You can tell at a glance which skills you have or have not introduced and/or reinforced.

Frank Schaffer's *Three Little Kittens* (FS-2352)

Literature Charts

Primary Picture Charts

Charts with pictures can help primary students function independently as they work on reading, literature, and other classroom activities. Be sure to take time to read each picture chart aloud and to tell students how they are used.

Trace your right and left hands on pieces of construction paper. Mount on the upper right and upper left corners of the chalkboard in the front of your classroom. This provides a left and right reference for students.

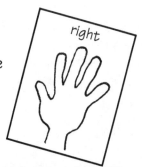

Charts of number words and color words can help K–1 students "read" independently. Make your own charts or use those that have been commercially prepared.

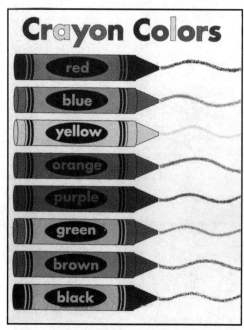

Frank Schaffer's *Crayon Colors* (FS-2434)

Frank Schaffer's *Numbers* (FS-2307)

Write directions words on a chart. Then draw pictures or paste objects beside the words. Or use a commercially prepared chart.

Frank Schaffer's *Read and Do* (FS-2304)

 # Notes